AVAILABLE NOW
from Lerner Publishing Services!

The *On the Hardwood* series:

Chicago Bulls
Dallas Mavericks
Los Angeles Clippers
Los Angeles Lakers
Miami HEAT
Minnesota Timberwolves
Oklahoma City Thunder
San Antonio Spurs

COMING SOON!

Additional titles in
the *On the Hardwood* series:

Boston Celtics
Brooklyn Nets
Houston Rockets
Indiana Pacers
New York Knicks
Philadelphia 76ers
Portland Trail Blazers
Utah Jazz

ON THE HARDWOOD

THUNDER

J.M. SKOGEN

On the Hardwood: Oklahoma City Thunder

MVP Books
2255 Calle Clara
La Jolla, CA 92037

MVP Books is an imprint of Book Buddy Digital Media, Inc., 42982 Osgood Road, Fremont, CA 94539

MVP Books publications may be purchased for
educational, business, or sales promotional use.

Cover and layout design by Jana Ramsay
Copyedited by Susan Sylvia
Photos by Getty Images

ISBN: 978-1-61570-515-3 (Library Binding)
ISBN: 978-1-61570-514-6 (Soft Cover)

TABLE OF CONTENTS

HAPPY NEW YEAR OKC

Chapter 1

A New Year

With ACDC's "Thunderstruck" blaring over the loudspeakers at Ford Center, the Oklahoma City Thunder took the court to an applause worthy of their name. Pride-filled energy pulsed through the crowd as they watched their home team—the newest team in the NBA—get ready to start the game. The new white, blue, and orange uniforms, only a few months old, now seemed so familiar. And the name, the Oklahoma City Thunder, was starting to roll off the tongue as naturally as the Boston Celtics, or the Miami Heat. Thunder fans could all agree on two things: One, they loved having a team of their very own. And two, the team was young, developing, and the city was optimistic.

Opening Night
OKC's New Year's Eve celebration is called "Opening Night," and has been around since 1987. Celebrating with the Thunder has become a new, and now unforgettable, part of this tradition.

This was not just a normal Wednesday night game. Fans flocked to the arena, cheeks still flushed from the cold December

A fan shows off his Thunder pride with a homemade sign.

7

air. They were not simply there to cheer for the Thunder, but to help ring in the New Year. Oklahoma City had a tradition of throwing a city-wide party to celebrate New Year's Eve. December 31, 2008, was no exception. There were concerts, a gala, snow tubing on the local ic[e] rink, fireworks, and even a "safar[i]" of baby exotic animals including [a] kangaroo and a lemur. And this yea[r] the city had a new addition to the[ir] holiday lineup. For the first tim[e] ever, OKC had a team that wa[s] in town to stay. Far[s] who went to the gam[e] were given a free pas[s] for other events late[r] that night all aroun[d] the city. Unfortunatel[y] many people figure[d] they would need a littl[e] cheering up at the en[d] of this game.

The Oklahoma Cit[y] Thunder were play[-] ing the Golden Stat[e] Warriors. The Warrior[s]

The Thunder's Kevin Durant fights for a New Year's Eve victory against the Golden State Warriors.

ad struggled on the road that season, which should have been good sign for Thunder fans. However, the Thunder had not had great start to their first season. With a record of 3-29, expectations were fairly low for the home team. Royce Young, a blogger covering the Thunder, summed up these negative feelings: "More than anything, tonight is about overcoming a mental block. The Warriors aren't necessarily more talented than Oklahoma City, but OKC can't seem to shake that it's supposed to lose." Fans were happy to fill the seats at Ford Center and cheer for their team, but there wasn't much hope for a win.

However, near the end of the third quarter the crowd was

Russel Westbrook is calm and focused during the last game of 2008.

delighted, and rather surprised, to find the Thunder up by six points. If their team could just hold it together for the final quarter, they had a real shot at victory. But the fans had

In the Right Direction
After starting their first season 3-29, OKC rallied and went 20-30 to close the year.

9

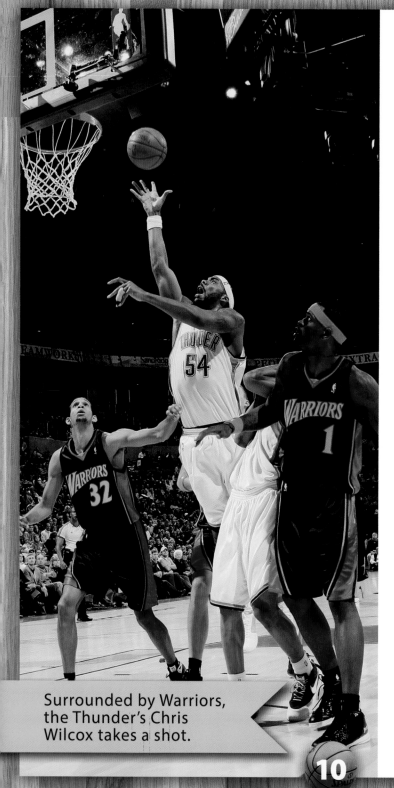

Surrounded by Warriors, the Thunder's Chris Wilcox takes a shot.

seen other games just lik
this earlier in the seasor
The Thunder would go int
the fourth quarter with
lead, only to crumble unde
the late-game pressure. S
it almost seemed natura
when, just a few second
before the third quarte
buzzer, the Thunder's Chri
Wilcox missed a slam dun
The ball spun off the side o
the rim, ready to be grabbe
up by the Warriors. This is i
fans thought. This was th
moment when the visitin
team would start chippin
away at the Thunder's lead
and their confidence.

But before fans coul
even blink, the Thunder

eff Green had scooped up the ball nd, in the next breath, launched imself into the air for a 15-foot mp shot. The swish of the basket, nd the crowd's cheers, ended the uarter. The Thunder led 78 to 70. here was still an entire quarter to o, but at that moment, ord Center was buzzing ith hope.

But the Warriors were ot done yet. By the seven-ninute mark, the visitors ere trailing by only three oints. Fans were once gain on the edge of their eats. The Thunder called a meout, hoping to recover he focus that had carried nem this far. Their coach, cott Brooks, must have

told them to start their New Year's resolutions a day early. When they hit the court again, it was with

Jeff Green flies toward the basket.

Coach of the New Year

At the time of this New Year's Eve game, Scott Brooks had only been interim coach of the Thunder for a little over a month. He was named head coach in April 2009. In 2010, Brooks was named Coach of the Year after leading his team to a 27-win improvement over the 2008-09 season.

victory in their sights. They played like a team that deserved to win, and they trusted each other to make that happen.

In one impressive show of team work, Earl Watson drove towards the basket and started to jump like he was going for a layup. Then, twisting in the air, he passed the ball to Russell Westbrook, who was waiting behind him. One of the youngest players on the team, Westbrook bounced the ball once and was off. There was so much air between his shoes and the hardwood, it was like he had springs glued to his feet. After making the basket, Westbrook gave Watson a quick high five. The Warriors played well, but they just couldn't close

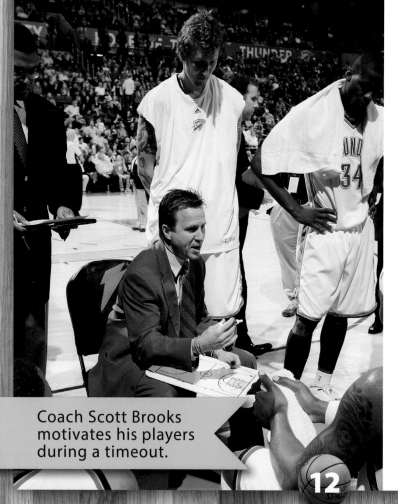

Coach Scott Brooks motivates his players during a timeout.

he growing distance in the score. The Thunder scored a 107-100 victory. Midnight was still a few hours away; but for the Thunder, a new year, and a new standard of basketball, was already here.

This game proved to be a turning point for the Thunder that first season. John Rhode, a reporter for the Oklahoman, wondered, "Perhaps a light suddenly came on inside the young minds of Thunder players. Perhaps they finally got it, or they believed in themselves, or they believed in each other, or all the above." The new year brought with it a new definition of the Thunder. The young, developing team was no longer in danger of breaking the record for the worst season in NBA history. They were learning

Almost there! Westbrook uses every inch of his 6'3" frame to score.

how to win, and they played like it. And Oklahoma City was given another tradition: The Thunder has won every single New Year's Eve home game since.

WELCOME TO THUNDER BASKETB

Chapter 2
HELLO, THUNDER!

Several years before the Thunder became Oklahoma City's team, the city had a test run with the NBA by hosting the New Orleans Hornets. OKC had never had a basketball team before. But they had an arena, and they had a lot of basketball fans who were eager for a home team. In January of 2005, a few months before the devastation of Hurricane Katrina, Mayor Mick Cornett flew to New York City. His goal was to let NBA Commissioner David Stern know how prepared Oklahoma City was for an NBA team. David Stern responded that hockey might be a better sport for the city. But the mayor's words and enthusiasm had left a strong impression on Stern.

A Warm Welcome

Commissioner David Stern traveled to OKC to watch the Thunder's first home game of the 2008-09 season. He addressed the crowd, saying: "Oklahoma City... welcome to the National Basketball Association."

Then, when the New Orleans Hornets were unable to use their home arena because of the destruction caused by Hurricane

Mayor Mick Cornett was a key player in bringing the NBA to Oklahoma City.

The Hornets take on the Grizzlies at Ford Center.

Katrina, Mayor Cornett personally gave David Stern a call. He told Stern that Oklahoma City would be honored to host the team. Though many other cities wanted the Hornets to play in their arenas, Stern decided to take a chance on Oklahoma City. From 2005 to 2007, Oklahoma City embraced the Hornets as their own home team.

They packed the stands—selling out games and letting the NBA know how ready they were for a permanent team. When the Hornets returned to New Orleans, many fans wished that they didn't have to leave. But most were happy that the Hornets were finally able to go home after such a terrible natural disaster. However, they missed the excitement of the games, and the pride that came with cheering for a home team.

To attract another NBA team, the people of Oklahoma City knew they would have to make significant changes to their arena. The city had already made great advancements around the Ford Center. Downtown OKC had been transformed from a rough area of town into a lively place with new restaurants, a movie theater, and an arena that still needed a bit of work. The Ford Center had been adequate when it was built a few years earlier, but it needed to be upgraded. Things like locker rooms, scoreboards, and concession stands needed to meet NBA standards. Berry Tramel, a

blogger for the Oklahoman, said that the Ford Center was "built on the cheap," and that the fans saw it as "functional, nothing more." But Oklahoma City didn't want to settle for "functional." They wanted an arena that would reflect their enthusiasm and their desire to have a permanent basketball team.

Ford Center at the start of the Thunder's first season.

17

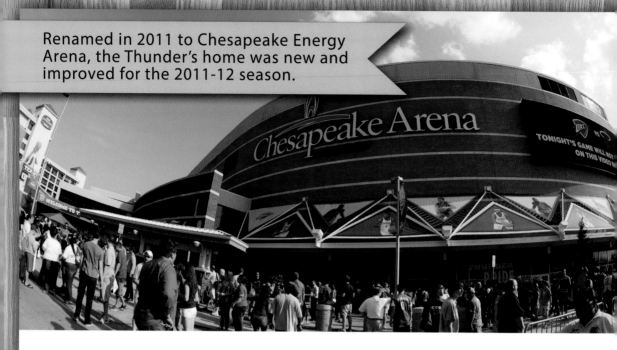

So the city took action, voting on a plan to improve Ford Center. Just a few of the changes would include a bigger entrance, new team locker rooms, rooftop gardens, and better suites. It would take years for all of the improvements to be made. But with this step, Oklahoma City declared itself to be a future home of the NBA. And, luckily for OKC, the NBA took notice. When owner Clay Bennett decided to move his team to another city, Oklahoma City had already showed that it was a community of eager fans, ready to embrace another team. They just wanted a team that would stay for more than a few seasons.

With the team beginning play in 2008, Oklahoma City had a lot of work to do. Before they could design uniforms, or plan the advertising, they needed to choose one simple yet very important thing—a name.

Clay Bennett wanted a name that not only reflected the strength of his players, but one that captured the spirit of their new home.

On September 3, 2008, at the team's headquarters in downtown Oklahoma City, Bennett climbed a podium. He was ready to announce the official name. Until this moment, all of the team's practice uniforms had simply read "OKC-NBA." The team was ready for a real identity, and in just a few minutes, everyone would hear the name, and see the official logo and colors.

There were hundreds of people gathered around, waiting to hear Bennett say

a name they already knew. A few weeks before this announcement, the name had been leaked, and even certain items were already listed on the NBA's online store. It wasn't just curiosity that drove all these people

OKC Thunder owner Clay Bennett addresses a crowd during the naming ceremony.

These six lucky kids are some of the first fans to wear a Thunder T-shirt.

The OKC Thunder's logo was unveiled to ACDC's "Thunderstruck"—a song that would become a kind of anthem for the team. A plain, black banner hung beside the podium, and it simply read, "Oklahoma City." Then, as the song began, the word "Thunder" being chanted over and over, the banner dropped away. A bright blue banner was revealed with the words "Oklahoma City Thunder," and the now-famous yellow, blue and orange-red logo beneath. Beside the banner, six children put on new blue T-shirts, all proudly displaying the team's logo.

Bennett had many reasons for choosing this name, and the colors

to come and listen—though they did want to make sure the rumored name was correct. They stood before that podium wanting to be a part of their team's history from the very first moment.

Local Color

The orange-red in the Thunder's team colors is also meant to be a mix of the local college team colors. The University of Oklahoma uses a crimson red, while Oklahoma State uses orange.

f the logo. The colors included the lue of the state flag, the yellow of he sun, and the reddish-orange f the sunset. The name "Thunder" was chosen to remind fans of Oklahoma's famous storms, and also their local history. The Army's 5th Infantry Division, based n Oklahoma City, were called the "Thunderbirds." A Thunderbird was a legend from Native American lore, whose wings could cause the wind to howl, and thunder to rumble.

This was exactly what Oklahoma City wanted—a team that would cause storms to rage, and make the earth tremble. And most importantly, they wanted a team that was entirely their own. When the season started a month later, Oklahoma City crowded into Ford Center to see the new uniforms, and chant their team's name. They were ready to be fans again.

This Oklahoma City man is ready for his first Thunder home game.

Chapter 3
NEXT YEAR STARTS NOW

Ford Center was full of bright blue shirts and a sense of wonder. Fans watched the Thunder battle the Lakers in the first round of the 2010 playoffs, another tangible step in the team's development. The Thunder had forced this series to Game 6. But the Lakers only needed to win tonight's game to move on to the next round. Looking back to just the previous season, when the Thunder had been in danger of breaking the record for the worst single-season record ever, this was an amazing accomplishment.

At the start of the 2009-10 season, there was every hope for an improvement over the last year's 23-59 losing record. In fact, when ESPN had predicted how each team would do in the coming season,

These opposing fans seem friendly now, but just wait until the game starts!

they had forecasted 32 wins and 50 losses for the Thunder. But no one besides Oklahoma City had thought that the Thunder would reverse that

Youth VS. History

2009-10 was the Thunder's first post-season appearance, but the Lakers were familiar with the playoffs—they had only missed the playoffs five times since the franchise started in 1948.

prediction, winning 50 games and losing only 32.

ESPN had also written about the buzz that surrounded the young Thunder, with such players as Kevin Durant and Russell Westbrook a ready showing great promise: "It not hard to see what the excitemer is about. But it will be hard to se them on TV." The Thunder only ha three nationally televised game in the regular season. But all 8 regular season games were broad cast on local channels to a hug number of fans—thos who weren't packing th arena in person. And o this particular night, th Thunder were *definitel* on national TV.

The Thunder hav also become a ver familiar sight to th people of OKC. Thunde players have made ove 900 visits to communit

Kevin Durant dribbles around the Lakers' Ron Artest on his way to the basket.

roups. Players rebuild omes in the city, lead clinics n obesity prevention, read o children, and distribute ee books—a lot of them. ia the Rolling Thunder Book us, the team has distributed 7,000 books to students hroughout OKC. In addition o free books, the Thunder layers also treat their oung fans to free tickets. he Tickets for Kids program ffers kids a chance to see

Kevin Durant offers advice to a youngster on the Rolling Thunder Book Bus.

heir favorite team in person. The hunder represent more than wins nd losses. The team also stands or their fans, and the organization akes sincere pride in positively mpacting the community every ay of the year, not just on game days. For all of these reasons, *ESPN the Magazine* recently ranked the Thunder as the number one professional sports franchise for fan relations. There is no question that the Thunder have become a vital part of OKC's community.

A True Survivor

A large American elm tree, called the Survivor Tree, resides at the Oklahoma City National Memorial. It was nearly killed by the blast, but it eventually bloomed again, and is now thriving.

The Thunder players wanted to embrace their new city just as much as the city wanted them. Even before the first season started, the player all took a trip to the Oklahoma Cit National Memorial. This memoria was built to honor the victims c the terrible bombing on April 19 1995, which killed 168 people. Thi was the worst terrorist attack in th United States until September 11

The Oklahoma City National Memorial has one empty chair for every victim of the attack.

001. Before the Thunder took he local spotlight with their nlikely winning season, that tack was what many people the country thought of rst, when they thought of klahoma City. The bombing still one of the top Google earch results for "Oklahoma", st after the Thunder, and he musical *Oklahoma!* The eam wanted to understand klahoma City's past, before hey become a huge part of heir future. And they wanted show their respect for what his great city had overcome. It has nce become a tradition for all ew players to visit the memorial efore they even start their first ractice.

The Lakers look on helplessly as the Thunder's Jeff Green makes a slam dunk.

Tonight's game was just over a week after the 15th anniversary of that horrible bombing. The people of Oklahoma City were making some serious noise, and earning

Winning around the World

In 2010, Russell Westbrook helped Team USA win gold at the FIBA World Championship of Basketball in Turkey. Before this victory, a USA team had not won gold since 1994.

Ford Center's nickname of Loud Cit
This had been a hard-fought gam
The Lakers were ahead for most c
the game, but with one second le
in the fourth quarter, th
Thunder found them
selves leading by on
point, 94-93. The Laker
Kobe Bryant had the ba
and was forcing his wa
up the side of the key. Th
Thunder's point guar
Russell Westbrook was de
fending him like a secon
shadow, planting himse
right on Bryant's hip. Bu
he couldn't stop Bryar
from taking a wild fade
away shot. Bryant threw
himself back, away fror
Westbrook, sending th

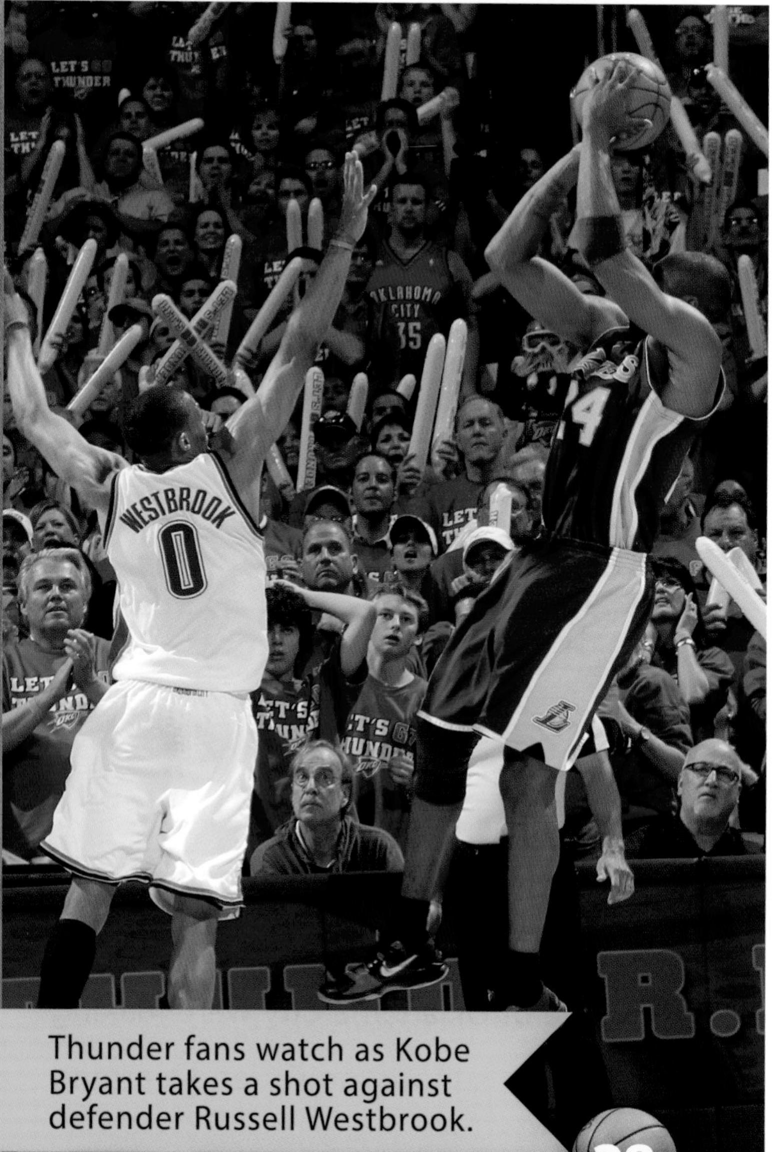

Thunder fans watch as Kobe Bryant takes a shot against defender Russell Westbrook.

all right towards the asket. The entire arena asped as it bounced off he rim.

For an instant, the rowd thought the hunder had defeated he mighty Lakers. They ould picture the ball lling to the ground, nd hear the buzzer gnalling victory for heir team. But the ball as snatched out of the r by the Lakers' seven- ot-tall forward center, au Gasol. When Gasol

Pau Gasol tips the ball in favor of the Lakers.

ammed that ball into the net, it was l but over. With half a second left n the clock, the Thunder attempted last, desperate shot. They passed Westbrook the ball, and he fired a lightning fast 23-foot jump shot from the very edge of the arc—and missed.

The players were devastated. Jeff Green bent over, holding his head in his hands. Kevin Durant fell to the floor and slammed his hands to the ground in disappointment. But the crowd—right after the buzzer marked the end of their team's second season, got to the feet and cheered. They stood there clapping and shouting and beating their thunder sticks as loud as they could. The Oklahoma City Thunder might have lost this game, but the city cheered for them anyway. The

Kobe Bryant shows his relief at the Lakers' victory. Durant does not hold back his disappointment at losing this key game.

tood while the two teams lined up and shook hands. And they kept standing, clapping, and roaring for their team for about 10 minutes. Because, when it all came down to it, this wasn't just their team anymore. The Thunder were a part of their city—a part of themselves. And they were so proud.

In the moments after this first round loss, Kevin Durant spoke to his team about how far they had come, and how far they would go. Durant told them, "Next year starts now." This comment must have sounded very familiar to the people of Oklahoma City. For the Thunder,

Kevin Durant gathers his team together for some encouraging words after the game.

and the entire city, a loss didn't mean the end of the world. With their strength and determination, it was only the beginning.

A Picture of Strength
Oklahoma City's mayor had a photo of Durant and Green leaning on each other after losing this game against the Lakers. To him, it represented the city's ability to overcome loss and make itself better.

The NBA blends the best athletes from all over the globe on 30 teams. The Thunder are a prime example of people with different backgrounds working together for a common goal. There was the slender shooter from Washington, D.C., and the lightning-quick point guard from Los Angeles who wasn't supposed to reach the NBA. There was the 6'10" shot-swatter from the Republic of Congo, and his bearded friend from Los Angeles. Four players, four different stories, and one goal in mind: an NBA Championship.

Kevin Durant was always a basketball player. Raised with the help of his

grandmother as one of four children in Washington, D.C., Durant spent his early years shaping his game alongside other current NBA players, like Michael Beasley, Ty Lawson, and

In 2007, while at the University of Texas, Durant was named NABC Division I Player of the Year.

33

Greivis Vasquez. Even among his peers, Durant stood out. In 2007, Durant and Greg Oden were not only two of the best college players in the nation, they were competing to be the number one pick in the 2007 NBA Draft. Oden eventually was selected before Durant so KD (Durant's initials and his nickname) would set out to Seattle to begin his career.

Durant did not start slowly. H[e] was Rookie of the Year in 2008, an[d] even more accomplishments, bot[h] personally and for his team, starte[d] rolling in from there. NBA All-Star[?] Check. NBA scoring champion[?] Check. All-NBA First Team? Check[.] NBA All-Star Game MVP? Check[.] Western Conference champion[?] Check. Olympic gold medalist[?]

Wearing their 2012 Olympic Gold, Kevin Durant and Russell Westbrook, along with the Heat's LeBron James, stand for the National Anthem.

heck. While Durant was always known as a "can't miss" kid for his sweet jump shot and the high odds that he would reach the NBA, his buddy from Los Angeles was less of a sure thing.

Russell Westbrook was 6'8" and a slim 140 pounds when he entered high school. He didn't even start for his varsity team until his junior year. Then, Westbrook started growing—and he didn't stop. When his senior year began, Westbrook had shot up to 6'3". But College offers were still not overwhelming. Westbrook enjoyed a bit of good fortune, though, when UCLA's point guard Jordan Farmar declared for the NBA Draft. All of a sudden,

Westbrook was thrilled to be on UCLA's team, and he still wears the number 0 for the Thunder.

UCLA needed a point guard, and they extended a scholarship offer to Westbrook. From there, Westbrook took care of the rest, eventually

In Remembrance

A childhood friend of Westbrook's, Khelcey Barrs, collapsed and died on the basketball court in 2004. Westbrook wears KB3, Barrs' initials and number, on a wristband to this day.

"Iblocka!" Serge Ibaka lives up to his nickname, blocking Pau Gasol's shot.

soon became known for h[is] basketball skills and for h[is] shot-blocking ability. H[is] nickname, 'Iblocka' instead [of] Ibaka, reflects the fact that h[e] led the NBA in blocked sho[ts] in the 2011-12 season. A[t] 6'10", Ibaka is a rim protect[or] defensively. His offensiv[e] game is developing nicely a[s] well, which was evident whe[n] Ibaka was a perfect 11-1[1] against San Antonio in Gam[e] 4 of the 2012 Western Conferenc[e] Finals.

joining Durant as an NBA All-Star and Olympic gold medalist.

L.A. is a long way from the Congo, so if Westbrook wasn't well-known, Serge Ibaka was even less so. Ibaka first had to distinguish himself in his own family, as he was one of 18 children. Ibaka

As far as scoring, James Harde[n] was instant offense. The NBA's Sixt[h] Man of the Year in 2012, Harde[n] was brought off the bench wit[h] the intent to score and creat[e] opportunities for the Thunde[r]

Beyond Harden's sweet jump shot, he has created quite a following with a beard that he's had since 2009. Too lazy to shave in college, Harden started growing a beard—which now has its own Twitter account and Facebook page. 'Fear the Beard' has become a popular saying in OKC. But even if opponents

Seeing Gold

James Harden was also on the 2012 USA Olympic Team, making the Thunder the first NBA team to send three of its players to the Olympics.

don't fear the beard, they must at least respect Harden and his three buddies, as they are the building blocks for an organization on the rise.

It is easy to recognize James Harden fans... just look for the beards!

WESTERN CONFERENCE FINALS

38

As the 2011-12 season opened, the Oklahoma City Thunder had only been in existence for four short years—a young team with young players. The "oldest" team in the NBA in 2012 was the Dallas Mavericks, with an average age of 30.33. The Thunder, on the other hand, were one of the five youngest teams, with an average age of 25.46 years old.

The Mavericks' Jason Kidd was 39 years old in the 2011-12 season.

Up until the 2012 Western Conference Playoffs, many critics thought the Thunder had a lot of potential. But they weren't convinced that the Thunder had the experience to be real contenders. For the past 13 years, only three teams had won the Western Conference Finals: the Los Angeles Lakers, the San Antonio Spurs, and the Dallas Mavericks. Could the Thunder really break that 13-year streak and go on

Get Well Soon!

Durant dedicated his 2011-12 season to former teammate Jeff Green. Green was traded to the Celtics in 2011, but was unable to play due to a heart condition that needed surgery.

to the NBA Finals? Oklahoma City fans cheered "Yes!" But much of the country thought that the Finals were still a few years away for this growing franchise.

But then the Thunder swept the Dallas Mavericks in the first round of the playoffs, knocking last year's NBA Champions out of the running. The rumblings began that maybe, just maybe, this young team might have a chance after all. Then they beat the Lakers in the next round and even crushed them by 29 points in the first game of the series. In two rounds, the Thunder had not only beaten the last two Western Conference Champions, but the last two NBA Champions. Now they would come face to face with the San Antonio Spurs.

Going into the Western Conference Finals, the Spurs had an 18-game winning streak. They also had been NBA champions four of the last 13 years. Many people

Durant takes a jump shot in Game 4 of the 2012 Western Conference Quarterfinals.

thought that the Thunder had had a great run, but there was little chance that they would actually win the series. The first two games began to prove those doubters right. The Spurs took the first two games in San Antonio. It looked like this might be a very quick series.

After those first two losses, the Thunder's coach, Scott Brooks, had the team sit down and watch video of their losing efforts. He wanted his team to watch their play, and figure out how they could improve. Brooks also wanted his players to point out the Spurs' weaknesses to prove that they were indeed beatable. They weren't about

Westbrook helps defeat the Lakers in Game 5 of the 2012 Western Conference Semifinals.

to risk a three-game-to-zero hole without first doing their homework.

At the beginning of Game 3, the Thunder and the crowd seemed to

Spurred to Success

Beyond winning 18 games in a row, the Spurs have another streak to their name. They've been to the playoffs every year since 1998, and have only missed the playoffs four times.

The Thunder's James Harden goes up against the Spurs' Tiago Splitter in Game 3

Mascot of the Year

Rumble the Bison makes over 400 appearances in the community every year. His home-game performances and community service made quite an impression on the NBA. He was named Mascot of the Year in 2009, his very first year as the Thunder's mascot.

feed off the each other' energy. The Thunde scored the game's firs eight points. For the fan who had come to watc the second Western Con ference Finals in OKC, thi was exactly the kind c game that they wantec The Thunder were i complete control. Durin a breathtaking play in th first quarter, Westbroo caught the rebound whe the Spurs missed a sho Westbrook passed it to Duran Durant slowly dribbled up the cour until he came to one of the Spur defenders at the top of the key Then Durant seemed to flip a switch and was suddenly accelerating. H drove the ball around the defender and up the side of the key. Then, with his feet never touching the paint, Durant flew through the air to the basket. He slammed the ball through the net, and the crowd exploded in amazement.

But the Spurs were not going to let the Thunder take this game without a fight. After making two free throws at the end of the first quarter, the Spurs were leading by two points. Could this be the beginning of the end for the Thunder in this series? The Thunder quickly gave the world their answer: absolutely not!

In the first two minutes of the

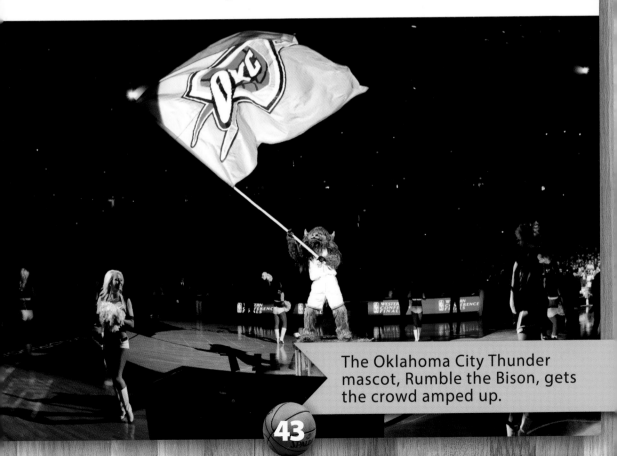

The Oklahoma City Thunder mascot, Rumble the Bison, gets the crowd amped up.

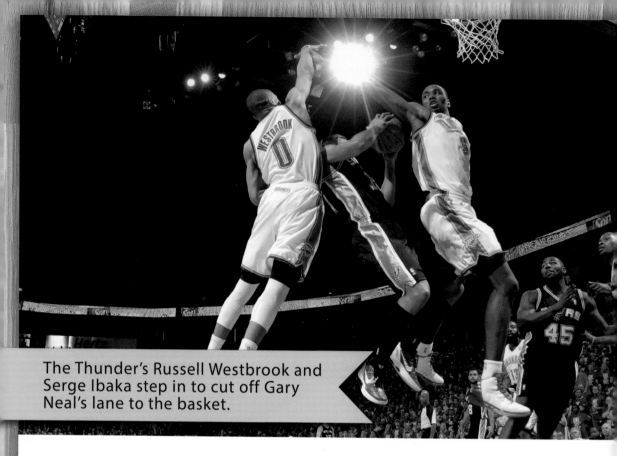

The Thunder's Russell Westbrook and Serge Ibaka step in to cut off Gary Neal's lane to the basket.

second quarter, the ball never seemed to leave the Thunder's hands. They put nine points on the board, firmly wrenching the lead away from the Spurs. And they never gave it back. For the entire second half of the game, the Thunder led by at least 10 points. The margin ultimately climbed to 20, with a final score of 102-82. The Thunder didn't just break the Spurs' winning streak; they shattered it all over the court.

When asked how the Thunder were able to make such a complete turnaround, Coach Scott Brooks responded: "We just played a good basketball game. We played with a lot of force, we played with good nergy, but we played defensive-minded basketball. That's who we re. That's how we win." This wasn't ust some mistake. The Thunder had earned how to take on the Spurs, nd they would use that knowledge o beat the Spurs in the next three ames. Now, for the first time, the hunder were Western Conference hampions. They were going to the inals.

Almost There!
For the past three years, the only teams to beat the Thunder in the playoffs were teams who went on to win the NBA Championship.

The Thunder won the first game of the Finals on their home court against the Miami Heat. Unfortunately, this was the last game that they would win in the 2011-12 postseason. The Heat took the next four games, sending the Thunder

The Spurs' defenders can't stop Kevin Durant as he soars to the basket.

Grace through the Loss

During the Thunder's last timeout of Game 5, Coach Scott Brooks told his team to hold their heads up high and congratulate the Heat like champions, because they deserved the victory this year.

back home to Oklahoma City without a trophy. But when the players arrived back in Oklahoma City, the were met by thousands of fans wh had gathered at the airport to gree them. This wasn't really a planned ce ebration, but still over 4,000 peopl came to show their love and suppor for their team. The Thunder player took turns address ing their fans, tell ing them that nex year they woul bring home the NB Championship. Bu for the thousand of beaming face in the crowd, the knew that they ha already won. Thi amazing, athleti beloved team wa here to stay.

Oklahoma City is always ready to come out and support its team.

46

Kevin Durant holds up the 2012 Western Conference Championship trophy.